Protecting the EARTH'S ANIMALS

Saving the Rainforests
Inside the World's Most Diverse Habitat

DIANE BAILEY

PROTECTING *the* **EARTH'S ANIMALS**

Saving the Rainforests

Inside the World's Most Diverse Habitat

BY DIANE BAILEY

Mason Crest

450 Parkway Drive, Suite D

Broomall, PA 19008

www.masoncrest.com

© 2018 by Mason Crest, an imprint of National Highlights, Inc.

Printed and bound in the United States of America.

Series ISBN: 978-1-4222-3872-1
Hardback ISBN: 978-1-4222-3880-6
EBook ISBN: 978-1-4222-7917-5

First printing
1 3 5 7 9 8 6 4 2

Produced by Shoreline Publishing Group LLC
Santa Barbara, California
Editorial Director: James Buckley Jr.
Designer: Patty Kelley
www.shorelinepublishing.com

Library of Congress Cataloging-in-Publication Data on file with the Publisher.

Cover photographs by Dreamstime.com/Keng Ho Toh.

QR Codes disclaimer:

You may gain access to certain third party content ("Third-Party Sites") by scanning and using the QR Codes that appear in this publication (the "QR Codes"). We do not operate or control in any respect any information, products, or services on such Third-Party Sites linked to by us via the QR Codes included in this publication, and we assume no responsibility for any materials you may access using the QR Codes. Your use of the QR Codes may be subject to terms, limitations, or restrictions set forth in the applicable terms of use or otherwise established by the owners of the Third-Party Sites. Our linking to such Third-Party Sites via the QR Codes does not imply an endorsement or sponsorship of such Third-Party Sites, or the information, products, or services offered on or through the Third- Party Sites, nor does it imply an endorsement or sponsorship of this publication by the owners of such Third-Party Sites.

CONTENTS

KEY ICONS TO LOOK FOR

Words to Understand: These words with their easy-to-understand definitions will increase the reader's understanding of the text, while building vocabulary skills.

Sidebars: This boxed material within the main text allows readers to build knowledge, gain insights, explore possibilities, and broaden their perspectives by weaving together additional information to provide realistic and holistic perspectives.

Educational Videos: Readers can view videos by scanning our QR codes, providing them with additional educational content to supplement the text. Examples include news coverage, moments in history, speeches, iconic moments, and much more!

Text-Dependent Questions: These questions send the reader back to the text for more careful attention to the evidence presented here.

Research Projects: Readers are pointed toward areas of further inquiry connected to each chapter. Suggestions are provided for projects that encourage deeper research and analysis.

Series Glossary of Key Terms: This back-of-the-book glossary contains terminology used throughout this series. Words found here increase the reader's ability to read and comprehend higher-level books and articles in this field.

INTRODUCTION

Imagine if you were dropped into the middle of a rainforest. A spider as big as a baseball scurries near your feet. Huge, colorful birds fly over your head. The ear-shattering howls of monkeys make you think you are most certainly not welcome here. But that green anaconda over there, her long, thick long body entwined in the branches of a tree, doesn't seem to mind your presence. She might invite you to come in just a little closer, for a hug . . . .

If you can escape the snake and ignore the monkeys (like the rare uakari, pictured at left), the amount to explore here is mind-boggling—but you'd better do it fast. By tomorrow, the patch of land you're standing on

Gorillas live in the African rainforest, Earth's second largest.

could be gone. That's like 75,000 football fields. With them, it's estimated they take more than 100 species of plants, animals, and insects.

And that's just in one day!

Tropical rainforests cover about 6 percent of the Earth's land surface (2 percent of its total surface). They're clustered around the Equator, which is threaded through the middle like a string holding it all together. Scientists estimate that about half the world's species live in these rain-forests. Some are so rare or specialized that they live only here and nowhere else. But people are steadily invading the forests, cutting down trees for timber and converting land to use for agriculture. Many animals are clinging to survival, in danger of becoming permanently homeless. Some have become extinct already.

But although a lot of rainforest has been destroyed, a lot still remains. People all over the world are working to save what's left—and everyone can play a part. If we act in time, it could help not only the animals that live in the rainforest, but the entire planet.

WORDS TO UNDERSTAND

biodiverse having a large variety of plants and animals in a particular area

ecosystem the places that plant and animal species live, and how they interact with each other and their environment

greenhouse gases gases in the air that trap heat and warm the atmosphere

poaching the act of illegally hunting animals

toxin a poison

LIFE IN A RAINFOREST

Fly over the ocean, and the view can get a little boring. It's just a big stretch of blue, and it doesn't look like there's much going on. You might think the same thing flying over a rainforest—it's just colored green instead of blue. But that's far from the truth. Just as with oceans, it's under the surface where things get interesting. Inside a tropical rainforest, each tree is like a skyscraper, with thousands of residents. The ones who live in a rooftop apartment may never cross paths with those who live on the ground floor. But all the animals here are important parts of the rainforest "city."

What is a Rainforest?

Hot and humid, warm and wet, steamy and sticky. There are lots of words to choose from, but they all describe a similar climate. By definition, tropical rainforests are watery places. They usually get at least 80 inches (203 cm) of rain each year, and the numbers can go up to five times that amount. The temperature also stays fairly constant, because seasons don't change much near the Equator. The thermometer usually reads somewhere between 70 and 90 degrees Fahrenheit (21 to 32 degrees Celsius).

A rainforest has a distinct structure with four layers. The highest, thinnest level is the emergent layer. Here, only the tops of the very tallest trees poke up, towering as much as 200 feet (60 m) above the forest floor. Not even the best of the climbing animals can make it this high, so only birds and flying insects live here. Below that is the canopy, the richest, most populated layer of a rainforest. This layer begins about 100 feet (30 m) above the floor and is roughly 30–40 feet (9–12 m) deep. Most sunlight doesn't penetrate beyond the canopy, so this is where plant life is most abundant. Lots of animals live here, too, because there's plenty of food for great apes and giant snakes alike. Beneath the canopy comes the understory, which extends to about 20 feet (6 m)

LAYERS OF THE RAINFOREST

Emergent Layer

Canopy Layer

Understory Layer

Forest Floor

above the ground. At the bottom is the spongy forest floor, littered with fallen leaves and branches.

Biodiversity

Scientists have known for years that rainforests are some of the most **biodiverse** places on Earth, with thousands of different species. But why is it that way? That's a trickier question. One idea is that a rainforest **ecosystem** is like a "cradle." It gives birth to many different species. Another is that it's a "museum," where species simply don't die out. Probably, it's some of both.

In either case, the rainforest environment is important. All living things need water, and there's plenty in a rainforest, so there's no competition for this resource. It's also warm all year long. Animals aren't dealing with problems like freezing weather that could kill them.

Poison dart frogs come in colors that warn predators.

Scientists disagree about how many animal species there are on Earth. In 1982, the American biologist Terry Erwin counted the number of beetle species that he found on a certain species of tree in the Amazon. There were more than 1,000 different types! Next, Erwin estimated the number of "specialist" beetles that would only inhabit that particular tree. Then he multiplied to figure by how many other specialist beetles and insects there would be on other trees in other rainforests. In the end, Erwin concluded the world could have 30 million different species of insects, spiders, and similar creatures—and that didn't even include larger animals! Since then, Erwin has said that the experiment was too small to make such a big conclusions. Scientists have revised the number to be about 7.7 million total animal species—but no one knows for sure.

Not that the rainforest is an "easy" place to live. There's a lot of water, but other resources can be limited. As a result, species must compete with each other. One strategy is to specialize. They might become the only species to eat a

Rainforests and climate change.

particular food, or they might develop a unique way to fight off predators. That's not always a peaceful process. For example, some scientists think that tropical trees and insects are in a constant race to out-evolve each other. Trees produce deadly **toxins** to kill insects that are munching on their leaves, and the insects in turn evolve new ways to resist and stay alive. This evolutionary leapfrogging leads to development of new species.

Something in the Air

During the process of photosynthesis, plants take in carbon dioxide and give off oxygen. More plants, more oxygen, right? It seems logical. That's why rainforests are sometimes called the "lungs of the planet." In this scenario, humans are the lucky winners because we need oxygen to offset all the carbon dioxide we make—not just through breathing, but also by burning fossil fuels like oil and natural gas. However, this equation is missing something. After plants die, they use up oxygen during the decay process, and give off carbon dioxide of their own. On balance, rainforests consume about the same amount of oxygen as they produce.

However, rainforest trees and plants are making an important contribution to the climate. Global warming is a big problem for the environment, and it seems to be getting worse. The ice caps at the poles are melting, and weather is becoming more extreme all over the world. Most scientists agree that humans are the main cause of global warming. Driving cars and burning fossil fuels for power plants

The dark green of rainforest treetops absorb sunlight.

create huge amounts of **greenhouse gases** that warm the atmosphere. Rainforests are helping out by acting like planetary air conditioners. The dense, dark-colored leaves in the rainforest absorb heat from the atmosphere instead of reflecting it.

Threats to the Rainforest

Unfortunately, tropical rainforests only occupy about half the amount of space they did several centuries ago. The rate of deforestation (complete destruction of a forest area) was relatively slow before 1850, but technology invented during the Industrial Revolution accelerated things. The population was growing, lifestyles were becoming more modern, and people wanted more stuff. This kept deforestation going at a fast pace all the way into the late 20th century. The rate slowed some in the 1990s and

Rubber tree farming occurs in several world rainforests.

Landowners in the Amazon burn or cut down too many trees.

early 2000s, but now is picking back up again.

Although rainforests took millions of years to evolve, they're now under attack from several factors—primarily humans. Deforestation for agriculture and logging destroys millions of acres each year. Climate change is also taking a toll. Hotter, drier weather puts stress on both plants and animals. Devastating fires are more likely to wipe out habitat. **Poaching** is another threat to some of the rainforest's more exotic animals.

All of this is contributing to the extinction of thousands of species, and scientists warn that we haven't seen the worst of it yet. When an animal becomes extinct, it's usually in response to events that have been happening for years. In general, animals that are smaller in size can survive lon-

Rainforests are very wet places, often linked to rivers.

ger as a species, because they require less space. Insects that are dying out in rainforests today are reacting to changes that may have begun a century ago. Large mammals, on the other hand, are more vulnerable. They are responding to more recent (and ongoing) destruction. In the coming years, the planet will have to pay its "extinction debt." The animals may still be alive today, but we will see them die out because they cannot recover from damage that has already occurred.

The rainforests aren't bankrupt yet, though. They're

shrinking in area, but there are also efforts all over the world to preserve what's left—and save the animals that are still hanging on. Each particular rainforest has its own animals to protect, but the challenges facing them are similar worldwide. In the following chapters, we'll take a look at the world's major rainforest areas, some of the animals that live there, and some of the threats they face.

 TEXT-DEPENDENT QUESTIONS

1. Why is there the most life in the canopy level of a rainforest?

2. What is one reason there is so much biodiversity in a rainforest?

2. How do rainforests act like air conditioners?

 RESEARCH PROJECT

Draw a picture or diagram of a rainforest, identifying the four layers. Now, choose one of the rainforest regions explored in this book, and fill in which animals from that region are found at each layer.

WORDS TO UNDERSTAND

ecotourism   a type of travel focused on seeing and helping to protect the environment

endemic   a plant or animal that only lives in a particular area and nowhere else

hydropower   electricity that is produced from the force of falling water

megafauna   extremely large animals

tributary   a smaller river or stream that feeds into a larger one

THE AMAZON

...ized past 50 years later,
the Sarasota Bay Dolphin Research
...uring 57 ...

Almost 50 years ago, in 1972, the Trans-Amazonian Highway (left) opened for traffic. It was 2,500 miles (4,000 km) long, passing straight through the middle of the dense Amazon Rainforest on its route across Brazil. Before the highway, the interior of the rainforest was difficult to reach except by foot or boat—and even then it was a challenge! For decades, people had been chipping away at small pieces of the rainforest, clearing trees to establish farms or ranches. But it was like scraping at a sticker on a piece of glass: the edges of the Amazon might be fraying, but the inner regions were mostly undisturbed.

The highway was a mark of progress. The

government of Brazil encouraged people to move in and use the vast resources of the rainforest to help the economy. Over the next 25 years, huge amounts of the rainforest were cut down to harvest rubber trees, mine gold, plant soy, or raise cattle. It came at a price. Animals that had lived here for centuries—from parrots and pythons to sloths and dolphins—were threatened as people carved up their habitat.

Mostly, the plan to move in and tame the rainforest did not work. Rainforest soil is poor in nutrients, and most new farms failed. By the 1990s the government of Brazil changed its focus and put a priority on conservation. The rate of deforestation slowed. It's still a battle, but the Amazon is probably doing the best of all the world's rainforest regions.

Pygmy tapirs are fighting to survive in the changing Amazon.

Sprawled through nine countries in South America, the Amazon basin still covers more than 3.1 million square miles (8 million sq km), of which 80 percent is forested. That makes it the largest intact rainforest on the planet. It's also a case study in how to manage a rainforest. The problems in the Amazon—and the solutions being tried there—are mimicked in rainforests across the globe.

Animals of the Amazon

Scientists estimate that about 10 percent of all the Earth's plant and animal species live in the Amazon. Many species are **endemic** to the region. There are pygmy tapirs and giant sloths, black caimans and red-faced uakari monkeys, pit vipers and pink river dolphins. The Amazon has an extraordinary level of biodiversity. But while 200-pound (90 kg) jaguars and 5.5-foot-long (1.7 m) giant otters still prowl the land and water, the Amazon is mostly known for its incredible array of smaller mammals, birds, amphibians, and insects.

There are an estimated 1,300 species of birds in the Amazon—about twice as many as in all of North America. The rainbow-feathered macaw and the big-billed toucan are easily recognized. There are also about 300 species of tiny

THE ANCIENT AMAZON

Twelve thousand years ago, the rainforests of South America were filled with large animals. There was *cuvieronius*, which stood seven feet (2.1 meters) tall and resembled an elephant. There was *glyptodon*, an armadillo that was roughly the shape of a ladybug and the size of a camping tent. Within a couple of thousand years, however, there were mass extinctions of these **megafauna**. More than two-thirds of animals weighing more than 22 pounds (10 kilograms) died out.

Scientists don't know what killed them, but there are still consequences after all this time. These ancient creatures plowed through the forest, devouring whatever was in their path, and left the digested remains behind. This excrement was rich in nutrients that helped the rainforest grow. After the largest animals went extinct, parts of the rainforest were starved of nutrients. It changed what types of plants and animals were able to survive, and how big they grew.

hummingbirds, and the powerful harpy eagle. This bird of prey has a wingspan of six feet (two meters) and dines on other forest creatures, including sloths and monkeys.

If the Amazon sounds like it's croaking, it might be because it is. About 10 million years ago, frogs began moving into the Amazon from the Andes Mountains on South America's west coast. Now there are about 1,000 species of frogs living here, and they look a lot different from the mud-colored amphibians of North America. Some are spotted; some are transparent. The red-eyed tree frog peers down from above, while the poison dart frog hops along the floor, safe from predators who recognize that its brightly colored body (it could be blue, orange, or yellow) means trouble.

With so much biodiversity, it's not particularly unusual for researchers to identify a new species, especially since animals in the rainforest are so specialized. Most newly discovered species are small, but occasionally a larger one emerges.

When a team of biologists explored the Amazon in 2011, they found a *titi* monkey, a 3.3-pound (1.5-kg) monkey about the size of a large kitten. That wasn't surprising—the Amazon is home to about 30 different species of titi, which can be distinguished by their long fur and tails. But this one was the wrong color. Other titis have gray tails, but this one had a bright orange tail, with fiery orange whiskers to match. After observing it more closely, the researchers determined the monkey did not belong to any of the 30 known species of titi. Instead, they had found a brand-new one.

An Endangered Ecosystem

Historically, the Amazon's best defense against people was its size and daunting geography, but that didn't last forever. As the 20th century drew to a close, it was clear that humans were making a dent in the rainforest—a big one. Millions of acres of forest were being cut down each year, and the list of endangered animals was getting longer.

Biologists and environmentalists saw what was happening and raised the alarm. Slowly, the governments of countries in South America began to listen. Bit by bit, regulations have been put into place to protect the rainforest. Most of the Amazon is located within Brazil, and in 1998, the country agreed to protect more rainforest land under the Amazon Region Protected Areas (ARPA) program. From 2003 to 2006, the amount of protected land doubled. It's still just a fraction of the total, though, and the effort has sagged in recent years. And other countries are even farther behind in passing (and enforcing) laws to protect rainforests. There's some progress, but it may be too slow to counteract the damage that's being done.

For instance, Peru has seen an increase in illegal gold mining near the Tambopata Reserve in the southeast area of the country. The price of gold tripled from 2008 to 2015, and thousands of eager miners swarmed into the region hoping to strike it rich. They have overturned tons of soil just to find enough gold to make a wedding ring. It's come at a huge environmental cost. Deforested areas can take hundreds of years to grow back. Plus, the area is now dangerously polluted with mercury that's used in the mining

Mining gold is a particularly destructive rainforest activity.

HEADING NORTH

Sometimes called the "Amazon of the North," the Great Bear Forest in British Columbia is a temperate rainforest. Temperate rainforests are located in the Earth's temperate zones, which are directly to the north and south of the tropical zone nearest the Equator. Most of these rainforests are found in coastal areas,

including the west coasts of parts of North America and South America, as well as Japan, New Zealand, and parts of northern Europe. There is only about one-sixth the amount of temperate rainforest as there is tropical, and they don't get as much rain overall. Temperatures are much more tied to the seasons, and you might need a jacket in the winter: although summer highs can reach about 80°F (26°C), the thermometer can drop to the freezing point in winter.

Canada's Great Bear Forest is home to animals such as cougars, gray wolves, and grizzly bears. One rare animal is the Kermode bear, a subspecies of black bear whose hair is not black but ivory-colored.

Bears have an important role in helping protect the rainforest. They have a diet heavy in fish, and after catching the fish, they often carry them deeper into the forest to eat. The leftovers rot, contributing nutrients back to the soil that help trees, plants, and smaller animals like worms and slugs. While all bears are good fishers, scientists think the white bears have an advantage. Fish have trouble seeing their white fur, so these bears catch significantly more fish than bears with black fur.

It's estimated there are only a few hundred (or perhaps even fewer) Kermode bears still living in the area, and they're at risk. Only about a third of Great Bear Forest is currently protected, and a proposed oil pipeline threatens some of the remaining area. The Kermode is popular among both locals and tourists though, and efforts to help the "Canada panda" may help preserve rainforest land.

PROJECT PIABA

Buy a fish, save a tree. That's the motto of Project Piaba (a type of fish that lives in the Amazon). The project operates along a 375-mile (600 km) stretch on the Rio Negro, a main **tributary** of the Amazon River. Here, local fisherfolk make a living by capturing freshwater fish like colorful cardinal tetras and cichlids. They're then sold to people all over the world who keep them in aquariums in their homes. Taking animals out of the rainforest  might not seem like a good way to save them, but in this case it's working. The fish reproduce quickly, and they're captured by hand, so the fishing process does not damage the environment. The money earned by selling the fish is enough to support many families who live in this area of the Amazon. If they couldn't fish, many say they'd turn to ranching or logging—both of which destroy the natural environment.

process. The mercury contaminates the food and water supply, threatening the entire food chain.

Effects of hydropower

Another intrusion into the Amazon ecosystem is **hydropower** projects. The power of rushing water can be channeled to produce electricity, and many sites in the Amazon's river system have been dammed to generate electricity. Advocates think it's an ideal way to jumpstart the economy, but some people are opposed. They argue that disrupting the flow of the river will wreak havoc with animals that live there.

An Eco-Economy?

Nobody would argue that saving rainforests and the animals that live there isn't a good idea in theory. But of course, there's a tradeoff. Some things that grow in the rainforest are definitely worth saving, such as rubber, bananas, coffee, and plants used to make medicine. But there's also a lot of money to be made by clearing the trees and using it for other businesses. Cattle ranching has been a huge threat to Amazonian rainforests, especially in Brazil. Cows need a lot of food, water, and space, which puts a lot of pressure on the rainforest. On the other hand, beef is

A good idea? Tourists feed the rare Amazon pink dolphin.

a high-priced export that brings in money.

The environment versus the economy—deciding which is more important is a tough question. Is there a way to satisfy the needs of both? More people are recognizing that in the long run, saving their natural resources may bring in more money than using them up. Rainforests are stunning natural attractions, and they're getting more and more rare. Many tourists are willing to pay top dollar to experience them—as long as they haven't been ruined. **Ecotourism** is a niche industry that serves travelers who are interested in visiting natural environments. People in the Amazon and Central America aggressively pursued ecotourism more than three decades ago. Now the idea has taken off in other parts of the world.

In Brazil, for example, cattle ranchers have branched out, running small hotels and offering guided walks or boat trips. This brings in money and motivates them to preserve rainforest areas. Jaguars, for example, are top predators in the

Amazon. Ranchers who work along the edges of the rain-forest battle jaguars that attack their cows. They view the big cats as nuisance animals. In the past, many wouldn't hesitate to kill jaguars to protect their livestock. However, that's at odds with tourists who won't pay money to see a cow, but are willing to pay for the privilege of seeing a jaguar up-close, in its natural habitat. Jaguars have gained a value of their own, and native people are less likely to harm them.

 ## TEXT-DEPENDENT QUESTIONS

1. Scientists found a new species of titi monkey in the Amazon in 2011. How was it different from other titis?

2. Name two industries that threaten Amazon rainforests.

3. Why do cattle ranchers sometimes kill jaguars?

 ## RESEARCH PROJECT

The Amazon River is an important part of the rainforest. It has two main seasons—regular and wet. During the flood season, the rainforest can be buried under 50 feet (15 m) of water. Find out more about how the river contributes to this ecosystem.

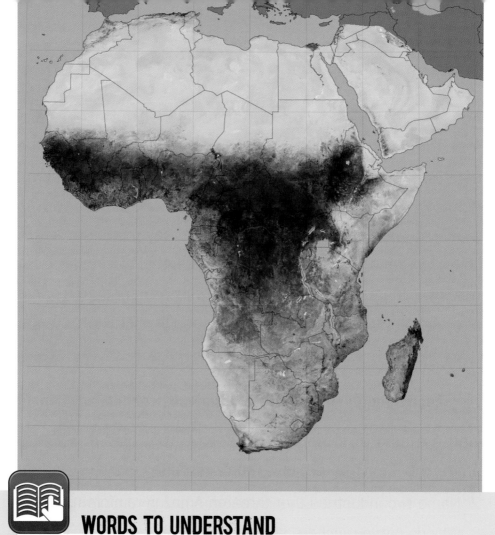

WORDS TO UNDERSTAND

bushmeat   food from the meat of wild animals

bribe   to illegally give someone money in exchange for a favor

expressive   able to show feelings or emotion

montane   related to mountains

refugees   people who have had to leave their homes due to war or natural disaster

savanna   a large grassy area with few trees

THE CONGO

Look at a geographical map of Africa, and it's as if you can actually see the heart of the continent. It's not red, but an uneven circle of dark green—the Congo rainforest. From here the land spills out into the patchy greens and browns of the **savanna** and then into the vast yellow expanse of the sandy Sahara Desert. But it is in that dense, vibrant patch of green that much of Africa lives.

Inside the Congo

At about 690,000 square miles (1.8 million sq km), the Congo rainforest is the second largest in the world. It spans six countries, mostly in The Democratic Republic of the Congo, The Republic of the Congo, Cameroon, and Gabon. The Congo is distinctly different from its Amazonian cousin. Most of it is at a higher altitude, and it doesn't get as much rain. The trees are taller, but overall the forest is less dense with vegetation. And although there are not as many different species, the Congo is home to some of the world's most spectacular rainforest dwellers. Many of the world's great apes—including gorillas, chimpanzees, and bonobos—live here. So does the okapi, which looks like a cross between an antelope, a giraffe, and a zebra. Crocodiles and hippos soak themselves in the Congo River,

The Congo River is home to thousands of hippos.

the world's deepest. And while you might picture herds of elephants roaming the grasslands of the savanna, forest elephants are a separate subspecies that likes to stick to the protected cover of the rainforest.

The Congo is also notable for its human population. About 75 million people live here—twice as many people than in the Amazon, even though the Congo is much smaller—and the population is growing. Many people are desperately poor, and they put a lot of pressure on the environment. They cut down rainforest trees for firewood and hunt **bushmeat** for food. Commercial operations in agriculture and logging (some of them illegal) also threaten the rainforest. Old-growth hardwood trees, like teak and wenge, are cut for their valuable wood. The cleared spaces are used to grow profitable crops like rubber trees, coffee, or sugar cane.

In addition, few places in the world are as politically unstable as central Africa. Decades of civil wars have led to corrupt and ineffective governments. In some cases, violence has driven people from their homes. They flee to areas where there are enough resources to support them—and that often means rainforests. After a brutal 1994 war in Rwanda, for example, 750,000 **refugees** set up camp in Virunga National Park in Zaire (now called The

KING OF THE JUNGLE

Lions usually live on the savanna, a fairly dry, open environment. So scientists with the Nature and Biodiversity Conservation Union (NABU) were surprised to find lions prowling around a **montane** rainforest in Ethiopia. This area is known for coffee, not big cats. Local residents claim to have known about the lions for a while. Even though the lions sometimes attacked their livestock, the villagers respected them as residents of the forest. When outside hunters came to eliminate "the lion problem," the villagers pointed the hunters in the wrong direction

to protect the lions. It's not known whether the lions live there permanently, because the area is a known route for migrating animals. Even if they're just passing through though, this small patch of rainforest that survives in Ethiopia is a welcome rest stop.

Democratic Republic of the Congo). Although the park's lands were legally protected, the refugees cared more about survival. They destroyed thousands of acres for firewood and killed wildlife for food.

Political problems make it difficult for African governments to enforce laws that protect the environment. Some people just ignore the laws. They **bribe** officials to look the other way. Violence is also not uncommon. Illegal poachers and loggers may hurt or even kill park rangers who try to stop them. Fearing for their own lives, the rangers may just let them go.

Historically, the Congo has had lower deforestation rates than other places, but the trend is now shifting. With more rainforest lands coming under the ax, animals that live there are increasingly threatened.

Gorillas

No animal symbolizes the African rainforest like the gorilla. People are fascinated by gorillas, probably because they resemble humans in so many ways, from their intelligence to their **expressive** faces. Unfortunately, all species of gorillas are on the endangered list. The main habitat for gorillas in the wild is spread over just 10 countries in western

This western mountain gorilla is facing extinction if not helped.

Africa. Since 2008, seven of those countries have joined the "Gorilla Agreement." This is a legal contract under which the countries agree to work together to protect gorillas by stopping poaching and preserving their habitat.

Ecotourism is one idea. People would pay to take trips to see gorillas, and the money would be used for conservation programs. Another idea is to discourage destroying old-growth trees in the rainforest just to be used for firewood. Instead, some organizations are building timber farms with fast-growing, low-value trees that are better to be used as fuel.

Efforts like these will only work if the greater habitat is preserved. In Nigeria, some conservationists are worried about a project that could undo a lot of good work. A proposed six-lane highway would run for 162 miles (260 kilometers), from the southern coast on the Atlantic Ocean into the interior of the country. Authorities hope it will help the economy by making it easier to move goods to ports. The route, howev-

ROAD TO DESTRUCTION

Protecting a habitat might seem to be fairly straightforward. Stay off, keep out, leave it alone, and everything will be fine. It's not that simple. Habitat doesn't boil down to just total acreage. It's also important that habitats be connected to each other. Imagine if you went to the park for a game of soccer, but there were only patches of grass as big as your bedroom, surrounded by huge mud pits. Technically, there's enough space, but because it's all chopped up, it doesn't do you a lot of good.

The challenge in rainforests all over the world is to focus on preserving large parcels of land, not just a lot of smaller ones. A fragmented habitat, crisscrossed by roads, separates animals (like the okapi, pictured) from each other. Roads also make their habitat more accessible to people. That puts them in danger from hunters, and makes it easier to set up farming or logging operations on pristine land.

MADAGASCAR

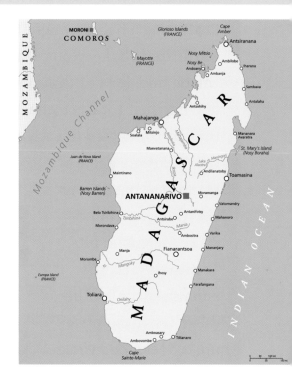

About 180 million years ago, most of the land in the Southern Hemisphere was connected in a huge supercontinent called Gondwana. The island now known as Madagascar was "smushed" in between Africa and India. Eventually the continent broke up, and by about 90 million years ago Madagascar had drifted off to become its own remote world.

Madagascar is the fourth-largest island in the world, and one of the most striking examples of biodiversity anywhere on the planet. Because it's some 225 miles (362 km) from mainland Africa, species here were isolated. They evolved differently than in other places.

Madagascar is especially known for its more than 100 species of lemurs. These types of primates evolved before monkeys and great apes, and now live almost exclusively on

Madagascar. Deforestation, mostly for firewood, is driving them out. Some species of lemurs are so particular about their habitat that they'll leave an area at the first sign of change. About 90 percent of lemur species are threatened, and almost a quarter are critically endangered. There's progress, though: in 2015, about 75,000 acres (30,300 hectares) were set aside for reserves, giving the lemurs some breathing room.

In the early 2000s, scientists thought the Madagascar Pochard was extinct. But in 2006, about 20 of these rare ducks were rediscovered. It had taken a while to find them, because they were living in a habitat completely un-like their old one. Biologists set up a breeding program to help the ducks increase their numbers, and by 2013, they'd grown to 80. They're still critically endangered, though, because their new habitat doesn't have enough food. Fortunately, biologists have their eye on a new spot, and are fixing it up so the ducks can move in.

er, would cut straight through the middle of Nigeria's Cross River National Park, as well as other protected reserves. Although the road itself would not take up that much room, it would fragment a sizable chunk of rainforest in Nigeria. It would prevent animals from moving freely around their habitat. Several animals are at risk, including chimpanzees, elephants, pangolins, parrots, and crocodiles. The one getting the most attention, though, is the Cross River gorilla. This subspecies of lowland gorillas is the most endangered great ape in the world. Only 250–300 individuals remain in total, and they are divided up into several small populations of only a few dozen each. It's critical that they keep what little habitat they have left. They also must have ways to move around easily and interact with each other. Unfortunately, the highway would likely divide the gorillas from each other even more. If they are unable to meet and breed, they will probably go extinct.

Cross River gorillas are one of the world's rarest animals.

Elephants on the Move

Cross River Gorilla

People have to do their part to save the rainforest, but animals can do some of the work too—if we'll just stay out of their way. In the Congo, large animals like elephants have a key role in keeping the rainforest ecosystem healthy. As they move through the rainforest, forest elephants trample the underbrush. If a small tree is in their way, they just wrap their trunk around it and uproot it! This creates paths through the forest that smaller animals use to get around.

The elephants are snacking on fruit as they go, distributing seeds through their dung that then grow into new trees. More than 300 species of trees in the Congo depend on elephants to scatter their seeds. If the elephant population drops too low, it could affect the number and types of trees that make up the rainforest. In turn, that will affect the populations of animals who have evolved to depend on them.

Unfortunately, the forest elephant is in grave danger. Elephants are listed as a protected species, but poachers don't care. They kill elephants for their ivory tusks, which can bring a lot of money on the illegal market. And because forest elephants are smaller and live exclusively in the forest, they are easier to hunt than their larger savanna relatives. One study shows that the population of forest elephants has dropped by about two-thirds since the early 2000s.

The elephants are also suffering from habitat loss, which is tied to the poaching problem. Elephants are smart enough to get out of danger when they can. They seem to understand what poachers are doing. When possible, if poachers move into an area, the elephants move *out*. That habitat still exists, but the elephants can't use it. They're now hiding from poachers, and are concentrated in only about a quarter of the territory they once occupied. The end result is similar to losing their habitat altogether. They need room to roam, and they don't have it.

The future of the Congo rainforest is still uncertain. Fifty

Elephants face disaster if poaching is not controlled soon.

years ago, rainforests covered the southern coast of West Africa, from Guinea to Nigeria. After years of battering from logging and agriculture, only a scant 10 percent remains in that area. The Congo is Africa's last large rainforest region. It will take hard work by conservationists, and a commitment from Africa's people and governments, to save it.

 ## TEXT-DEPENDENT QUESTIONS

1. How do political problems put rainforest habitats at risk in Africa?

2. Why would a proposed highway in Nigeria threaten the Cross River gorilla?

3. How do elephants help maintain the forest environment?

 ## RESEARCH PROJECT

Ecotourism is one way to raise money and awareness for conservation projects, but it has downsides, too. Research how tourism could be used to help gorillas or elephants. Make a list of the pros and cons. What do you think—is it a good idea?

WORDS TO UNDERSTAND

herbicide a poison used to kill plants

invasive in biology, describing a species that invades an area where it is not native

pulpwood wood that is grown to be made into paper

secondary forest a forest that grows in the same place as one that has been cut down

RAINFORESTS IN SOUTHEAST ASIA

Dip a paintbrush in some bright green paint and fling it across a canvas. The result might resemble the rainforests of Southeast Asia. They're dotted across the southern Asian mainland and onto the thousands of islands stretching from the eastern Indian Ocean to the western Pacific Ocean.

These rainforests present a much different picture than those in South America or Africa. They're patchier, smaller, and older. Some of the world's most famous animals live here, but they are huddling in ever-smaller areas, in ever-smaller numbers. The thick rainforest that covered the area just a century ago is quickly balding as humans take over.

Paper and Palms

Printer paper. Tissue paper. Paper towels. Notice a theme here? It's this: orangutans don't use any of these things. And unless they start writing reports, blowing their noses, and cleaning kitchens, they may get less out of their natural habitats than ever before.

Once, orangutans were sprawled across many of the islands of Malaysia and Indonesia. Now they live in just two places, the large islands of Borneo and Sumatra. It's difficult to count them exactly, but biologists estimate that only about 50,000 Bornean orangutans remain. Next door, on the island of Sumatra, the Sumatran orangutan is much worse off. Only about 7,000 individuals survive there. Both types are endangered.

Forests used to blanket these islands almost from coast to coast, and tree-loving orangutans could travel wherever they wanted without ever setting foot on the ground. Now, only a fraction of this ancient rainforest is still intact.

The trees were more than an elevated highway for orangutans who wanted to swing through the branches instead of walk. Much of this native forest was filled with trees called dipterocarps. These trees produce fruit that orangutans love. Unfortunately, they are also useful to humans. First,

JUNGLE SCHOOL

Don't be late! At this school on the island of Borneo, nobody misses the bus—or in this case, the wheelbarrow. These students are young orangutans, and a worker at this animal rescue facility takes the animals to their daily classes in a wheelbarrow. In the long run, saving rainforest habitat will be a key part of saving orangutans. But right now, the problem is

too important to focus only on long-term approaches. Environmental groups are stepping in with aggressive measures to save orangutans, especially young ones. If volunteers find them orphaned or stranded, they take them in and send them to "jungle school." Here, the orangutans are coached in basic survival stuff, including climbing trees, finding food, and avoiding predators—including people. Once they've got it down, they "graduate" and are released back into the wild.

dipterocarp wood provides valuable timber. Once the land is cleared, it can be used to raise **pulpwood** trees. These are low quality and can't be used for lumber for building, but they grow fast and are good for making paper products.

Other forest areas are being cleared to create plantations for oil palms. The oil from these trees has several uses in food, fuels, and cosmetics. Oil palms grow well in the nutrient-poor soil of rainforests, and they don't need a lot of care. They can be a lifesaver for small farmers, but they're also pushing out old-growth forests.

Is there room to make a deal? Conservation groups want to preserve pristine rainforest areas, but they're also open to compromises. For example, the World Wildlife Fund works with timber companies so that they don't clear-cut an entire area, leaving nothing standing. Instead, only some trees are taken, and some are left behind to provide original habitat and food sources for the orangutans.

Customized Conservation

The Ujung Kolon National Park, on the western tip of the island of Java, is connected to the Java mainland by just a small knot of land. This peninsula is the world's last remaining refuge for the Javan rhinoceros, but it's a mixed

Captive breeding of the Javan rhinos might help them survive.

blessing. Ujung Kolon is geographically isolated from the rest of the island, which provides some protection. Conservationists work hard to make sure human activities outside the park don't spill into it, and hunting and logging are banned. In 2010 and 2011, authorities persuaded farmers living there illegally to move out.

That's all good, but there's only so much space in the park, meaning the rhinos don't have much room to grow. They are cut off from moving into other areas where they could expand. Worse, the habitat is under threat from the **invasive** Arenga palm. This tree grows everywhere, and it's squeezing out the plants rhinos traditionally eat. (Rhinos aren't picky eaters. They'll eat about 200 different kinds of plants, but the Arenga palm isn't one of them.) The International Rhino Foundation, which works to preserve the animals, estimates that only about 40 percent of the park is useful habitat at this point. Even if there were more rhinos, there isn't enough food to go around.

Conservationists are working on some jungle gardening. They've experimented with ways to eradicate the Arenga palm in the rhinos' habitat, either by cutting the trees down or by treating them with **herbicides** that will kill them. It seems to be working.

This little Arenga palm could be harming rhinos.

Across the Sunda Strait between Java and Sumatra, the Sumatran rhino also faces problems. As rhinos go, they're small—usually less than 2,000 pounds (907 kg). It's estimated there are fewer than 100 of these animals left on Sumatra and Borneo, with a few others living in zoos around the world.

The Sumatran rhino has habitat issues, too, but they're different from those of the Javan rhino. While the Javan rhinos are clustered together, the Sumatran rhinos are scattered about the island. Coffee and rice plantations have fragmented their habitat so much that the rhinos rarely cross paths. That makes breeding unlikely.

Helping Javan rhinos

Bringing it Back

Almost a century ago, scientists had a bold idea. The rainforests in Southeast Asia were already shrinking, losing out to timbering, agriculture, and other human activities. But if people could take it away, could they also bring it back? In 1926, authorities began replanting forests in Malaysia. The idea had an economic basis—grow trees in order to cut them down later. But within a few decades, scientists were looking at the results from an environmental standpoint, trying to assess the overall health of the forest.

Fast-forward 90 years. Today, this **secondary forest** looks much the same as the primary forest around it. There's a big difference, though. It lacks the biodiversity of old-growth forest that was never disturbed. Scientists think the diversity will come over time—but it will take closer to 1,000 years, not 100. After all, growing trees is just one part of growing an ecosystem. In other places, where reforestation occurs naturally, the process can take much longer. In parts of Cambodia and Central America, for example, forests were destroyed during wars that were fought more than 500 years ago. They still haven't fully recovered.

There's some good news, though. Studies have shown that many species can exist in secondary forests. Orangutans prefer primary forest that has not been damaged, but they can make do in secondary forest, at least for a while. Sumatran rhinos are also drawn to secondary forest. Brushy undergrowth is thicker where tall trees have been cut, so they can get plenty of food. Reforestation isn't the answer to keeping the forests intact in the first place, but it may help.

Can this orangutan's home be saved by humans?

Looking to the Future

What would the world be like if hundreds of species of animals went extinct? At the least, it would be a poorer place. It could cause problems with entire ecosystems and with the planet's climate. It might have consequences we can't even foresee, that go far beyond the borders of the rainforests where those animals lived. Fortunately, people all over the world are stepping up to save them.

Rainforests are still mysterious places. It takes a lot of nosy scientists to uncover their secrets. In many cases, we do not even know exactly who or what we're trying to save! But we do know that we had better act quickly. If we don't, we might never have the chance to find out what else the rainforests are hiding.

 ## TEXT-DEPENDENT QUESTIONS

1. What two islands do orangutans live on?

2. Why is the Javan rhino running out of food?

3. Why did Malaysian authorities start a reforestation project in 1926?

RESEARCH PROJECT

Historically, the Asian rainforest was bigger, providing more room for large animals like elephants and gorillas. Look up maps that show the spread of the rainforest a century ago compared to now. If you could draw connecting corridors to help animals be able to move around, where would they be?

You may not live anywhere near a rainforest, but there are still things you can do to help protect rainforests and the animals that live there.

Remember the three R's. That stands for reduce, reuse, and recycle. Cutting back on how much you consume is a small step that anyone can take. Put everyone's efforts together, and they can help slow the rate of rainforest deforestation.

Be Fair. People eat all kinds of things that come from rainforests. "Fair trade" foods are produced in ways that treat local workers fairly and help the environment. Look for foods that have been fair-trade certified—coffee and chocolate are two of the big ones. Poaching is also a problem for rainforest animals. If you buy something made from animal products, make sure you research where the item came from, and that it didn't hurt an endangered animal.

Adopt an Animal. With so many animals living in the rainforest, it would be hard not to find one that strikes your fancy, and there's probably an organization working on its behalf. Pick one you like and read up on what's being done to help it. Many groups

welcome volunteers, and for a donation you may be able to "adopt" an individual to help keep it safe.

Do the Job. Saving the rainforests isn't a big job—it's lots of big jobs. Whatever your skills, find ways you can pitch in. If you like biology, botany, or ecology, you could study the science of rainforests. There are also jobs for people who work in government or other organizations, helping to make policies or set up local programs.

Speak Out. It can take a while to make changes—especially at an international level! But when enough people make their voices heard, things can go a little faster. Sign petitions and write letters or emails to people or organizations that have the resources to help save rainforests.

FIND OUT MORE

BOOKS

Eckhart, Gene, and Annette Lanjouw. *Mountain Gorillas: Biology, Conservation, and Coexistence*. Baltimore: Johns Hopkins University Press, 2008.

Jackson, Tom. *Eyewitness Amazon*. New York: DK Publishing, 2015.

Tarbox, A.D. *A Rainforest Food Chain (Odysseys in Nature)*. Mankato, MN: Creative Paperbacks, 2016.

WEBSITES

www.nature.org/ourinitiatives/habitats/rainforests/index.htm
The Nature Conservancy's rainforest page collects news and information about rainforest conservation.

www.nationalgeographic.com/environment/habitats/rain-forests/
The famed nature magazine has a site with lots of rainforest information.

www.wildnet.org/
The Wildlife Conservation Network focuses its efforts on endangered animals around the world, and, of course, rainforests.

SERIES GLOSSARY OF KEY TERMS

acidification the process of making something have a higher acid concentration, a process happening now to world oceans

activist someone who works for a particular cause or issue

biodiverse having a large variety of plants and animals in a particular area

ecosystem the places where many species live, and how they interact with each other and their environment

habitat the type of area a particular type of animal typically lives in, with a common landscape, climate, and food sources

keystone a part of a system that everything else depends on

poaching illegally killing protected or privately-owned animals

pollination the process of fertilizing plants, often accomplished by transferring pollen from plant to plant

sustain to keep up something over a long period of time

toxin a poison

INDEX

PHOTO CREDITS

Adobe Images: Antoine Ede 20, Noradoa 37, Peter Hermes Furian 44, Lilian 58. Alamy Stock Photo: blickwinkel 32. Dreamstime.com: Louis Louro 6, Grodza 8, Kleinermann82 12, Dirk Ercken 14, Antonioclemens 15, Salparadis 17, Airubon 18, Andre Costa 19, 20, Ecophoto 40, Henner Damke 42, Mohana Antonmeryl 43, Andre Gudkov 48, Alan Webber 50, Mihaic 55, Ponsulak 56, Flair Images 60, scanrail 61, Joanne Zheng 62. Dublin Zoo: 24. International Animal Rescue/SWNS: 53. Shutterstock: Dr. Morley Read 10, Ryan S. Bolton 29. Wikimedia: HTO 26, Maxmilian Helm 32, Redheylin 36, 45, Julielangford 46.

ABOUT THE AUTHOR

Diane Bailey has written dozens of non-fiction books for kids and teens, on topics ranging from sports to science. She has two sons and lives in Kansas.